POETRY

How to Kill Poetry
Road Work Ahead
Mute
This Way to the Acorns
St. Michael's Fall

FICTION

Men with Their Hands

NONFICTION

From Heart into Art: Interviews with
Deaf and Hard of Hearing Artists and Their Allies
Notes of a Deaf Gay Writer: 20 Years Later
Assembly Required: Notes from a Deaf Gay Life
Silence Is a Four-Letter Word: On Art & Deafness

DRAMA

Whispers of a Savage Sort and
Other Plays about the Deaf American Experience
Snooty: A Comedy

AS EDITOR

QDA: A Queer Disability Anthology
Among the Leaves: Queer Male Poets on the Midwestern Experience
Eyes of Desire 2: A Deaf GLBT Reader
When I am Dead: The Writings of George M. Teegarden
Eyes of Desire: A Deaf Gay & Lesbian Reader

★ THE KISS OF ★
Walt Whitman
STILL ON MY LIPS

Raymond Luczak

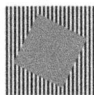

Squares & Rebels
Minneapolis, MN

In Gratitude

The author is most grateful to: Bryan Borland, John Lee Clark, David Cummer, Jameson Currier, Bambi Gauthier, Jill Gerard, and Chael Needle for their editorial support; Eric Thomas Norris and Dan Vera for their generous words; A. Mars for his modeling beauty; M. Nicolas Silva for his flattering picture; and Arthur Durkee for his lovely "Song of Walt."

Justin Martin's *Rebel Souls: Walt Whitman and America's First Bohemians* and Matt Miller's *Collage of Myself: Walt Whitman and the Making of Leaves of Grass* proved to be revelatory. Along with Whitman's own *Leaves of Grass* (particularly the 1856 edition), Gary Schmidgall's books *Walt Whitman: A Gay Life* and *Walt Whitman: Selected Poems 1855-1892* provided endless inspiration.

Acknowledgments can be found on page 94.

Copyright

The Kiss of Walt Whitman Still on My Lips.
© Copyright 2016 by Raymond Luczak.

Author Photograph: M. Nicolas Silva.
A. Mars Photographs: Raymond Luczak.
Walt Whitman Images: Library of Congress and Walt Whitman Archive.
Cover Design: Mona Z. Kraculdy.

All rights reserved. No part of this book can be reproduced in any form by any means without written permission. Please address inquiries to the publisher:

Squares & Rebels
PO Box 3941
Minneapolis, MN 55403-0941
E-mail: squaresandrebels@gmail.com
Online: squaresandrebels.com

Printed in the United States of America.
ISBN: 978-1-941960-03-5
Library of Congress Control Number: 2016900301

A Squares & Rebels First Edition

"I have the kiss of Walt Whitman still on my lips."

—Oscar Wilde, in a letter to George Cecil Ives,
after meeting Mr. Whitman in 1882

... And your very flesh shall be a great poem.

for S.W.G.

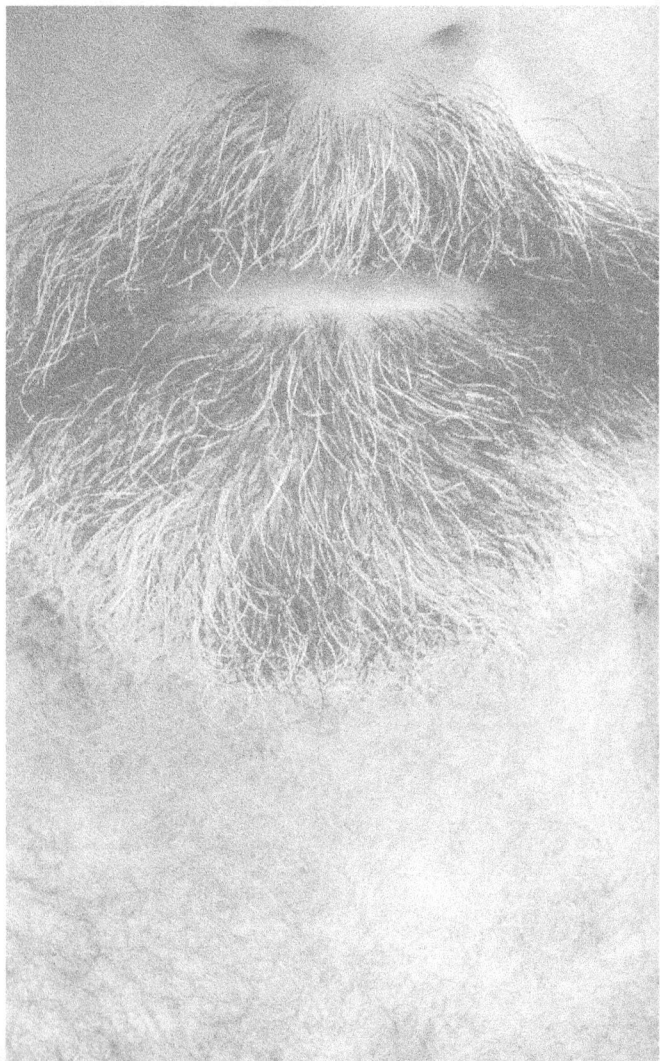

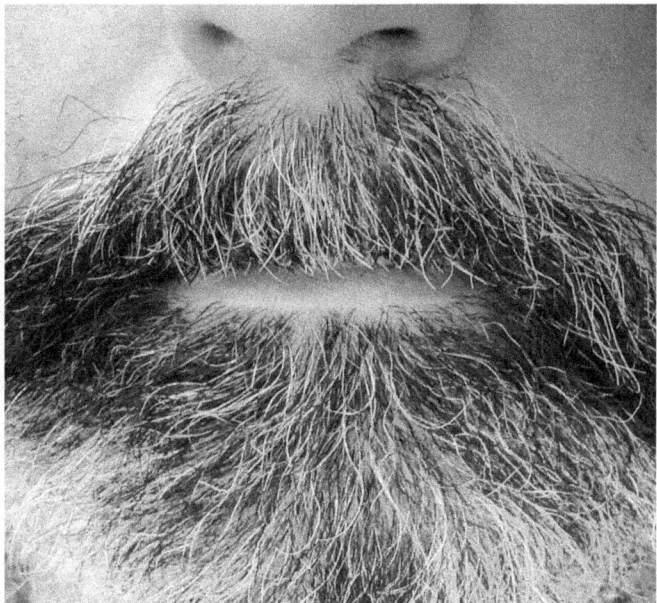

I.

Here! take from my lips this kiss,
Whoever you are, I give it
especially to you ...

THE KISS OF WALT WHITMAN

In his hands are my blood petals withering,

its brown edges shriveled fingernails.

The grass is a bed of green thorns.

Blue jays peck deftly at helpless worms.

Spider mites whiten a croton's armpits.

Crows puncture the skin of a gray squirrel.

Daffodils hide their yellow eyes in shame.

I've been without water all season.

I lose color when he flings outward the petals.

STILL ON MY LIPS

My leafy voice is lost, rubbed raw

with bitterness of lemon, stringiness of celery,

and bites of radish. I can't sing for my salad.

A cold stranger a long time ago tossed my voice

into the compost heap. It took me years

to sift and make it fit. My throat gurgles

with beetle wings clipping my vocal cords. I've

a Frankenstein's monster bass voice fit for the undead.

Silence is my best piece of music.

THE KISS OF WALT WHITMAN

Thousands of seeds have passed through the furrows

of his hands. They leave the comfort of his palm

as he thrusts a finger into the crack of earth

down the assembly line. He prides himself

as a factory worker of sun and rain.

He wipes his brow with the hem of his t-shirt.

His pectorals are mossed with peat-fur

as the dew of sweat lines his waist. He glances

up at me, not seeing how anointed I've become.

STILL ON MY LIPS

Just like how some men like to compare their dicks,

he and I compare our beards. Though eight years older,

his beard is darker, thicker, dense. Amidst his prattle

about his favorite painters (Vermeer and Leonardo),

Corinthian columns, and Cate Blanchett in *Elizabeth*,

he peers closely at my beard: once a fiery red,

now a cropped ginger mellowing into ashy white.

I await the flame of question in his eyes.

My answer is ready: yes, *you can fondle my beard*.

THE KISS OF WALT WHITMAN

I long to photograph him, his beard jutting out

proudly, his hand firmly ensconced over his heart,

standing like the flint-scarred Civil War veterans,

having seen bodies of their buddies strewn

dead. Yet I remain alive in his presence.

Each time I blink, my mind's camera shutters

the sunlight brushing her lips against his.

My lens flirts with setting off memory's dynamite,

its glass shattering upward into a nebula sighing.

STILL ON MY LIPS

Chest against chest: the armor plate of war,

removed, is soft, easily bruised. Army tank

fingers roll up and down dunes of nipple.

Beard against beard: the nerve endings

of desire rake across the long grasses

as fingers interlock like combs. We moan for surrender.

Tongue against tongue: the only tug of war

everyone wins when they all fall back on the bed.

But nothing of the sort happens. He has to leave. Again.

THE KISS OF WALT WHITMAN

In my arms is a rumble of calamus

torn from the soggy marsh, tired of toads

leaping up for nothing and waving blades.

I chew on its pink roots to freshen my breath.

But it's not enough. I need his tongue

to disinfect my mouth of untruths,

licking my body clean of swampy sweat.

His firefly eyes do not see me.

Cattails knock each other in the night.

STILL ON MY LIPS

Dragonflies weave in and out of the dank swamp

where mosquitoes punch in their timecards

every other second when they scent blood,

only to be shuttered away by the razor ears

of bats slicing the night air with nary a *tsk*.

My boyhood was an endless elegy to moths

ensnared in the unexpected trap of naked lightbulbs.

I learned early not to flex my wings too much.

I had to freeze the ache of summer with winter eyes.

THE KISS OF WALT WHITMAN

Deafened at the age of eight months, I learned to hear

through the stainless steel shells of my body aids

shoehorned into my harness bra. I was an analog cyborg.

I learned to speak from feeling the vibrations

in my speech therapist's throat, and mine too.

My nasal sandpapery voice singles me out in a crowd.

Using the language of hands was forbidden.

Until I learned Sign, I had to make do with watching

the mystery and misery of lips masticating words.

STILL ON MY LIPS

When I need a reprieve from lipreading,

I call upon memories of heading into the woods

across the street from the house where I grew up.

There, nature sang songs I could hear perfectly

without my hearing aids. I lay there, quaking naked

on a beach towel, afraid of being caught and yet

yearning for this or that man I'd spotted earlier that day.

Sparrows, strung along on power lines cutting a swath,

never flittered about the pearls of peace in my hands.

THE KISS OF WALT WHITMAN

While in college, I tranversed endlessly Dupont Circle's

spoke-streets radiating out in Washington, D.C.

I learned to speak the language of lust

with my eyes. No one taught me how to approach

a carpenter hauling his toolbox into his truck

or a shy Ph.D. student coming out of an used bookstore.

With our eyes trailing up and down each other's body,

I learned to ask questions like "Where you headed?"

The electricity between us made me sing.

STILL ON MY LIPS

Yet silence fails to convey the full volume

each time he shows up at my door.

His brown absinthe eyes stir desire,

a *Reader's Digest* condensation of Tolstoy

that requires no translation. Eyes, always

a language of impossible phrases,

bypass regions of the brain that demand logic.

I thirst for his monkey moonshine,

but by the time he sits down, he's all out of drink.

THE KISS OF WALT WHITMAN

Stories are all he's got to offer as a guest.

But his beginnings are fractured, ceramic

cookie jars fallen on the kitchen floor.

His rambling middles are plot developments

so slight they pass by in a blink of the eye.

He leaves me hanging for the unresolved,

to be continued at the oddest times.

I offer him raspberry lemonade. He sips.

Fortune cookies are another form of prayer.

STILL ON MY LIPS

Hours later he leaves. My pitcher's empty.

I wash dishes and stand them in the sink rack,

where tears drip dry of what I'd hoped to feed,

collecting instead in the drain of my soul.

He said he's had only three dates in five years.

I am silt sludging in the cesspool of my heart.

Unrequited affections make the worst toxins.

There's no safety left in the river I must swim.

Catfish slither unbidden in the murk.

II.

Hands I have taken, face I have kissed,
mortal I have ever touched,
it shall be you.

THE KISS OF WALT WHITMAN

Walt, I dreamed of you and I together sleeping,

beards commingling and bodies clinging,

hands entwined and legs enmeshed,

twin plants woven together from the same pod

sown deep by a gardener who understood

the need for pearly drops of morning rain

sheathing our man-roots in the night

so that by day we could walk bright as rosebuds,

ready to unleash again the comradeship of musk.

STILL ON MY LIPS

You spoke in clangorous lines as long as trains

hurtling deep in the guts of mountains,

rattling and careening between the two rails,

leaving behind farts of coal smoke,

darkening the tunnel walls with a layer of soot.

Out on the Great Plains the prairie grass waved

at oceans of grain, locusts a memory.

The blue skies were bigger than deemed possible.

America's arms were big enough to cradle you.

THE KISS OF WALT WHITMAN

From across what little you'd seen of America,

you catalogued, celebrating all from manure to semen,

even appraising wind's "soft-tickling genitals."

Mannahatta was its crown jewel of industry,

spilling forth diamond eyes of young men

gleaming in the velvet darkness among their kind.

Rings of kisses and gropes were sacrosanct

behind the shuttered eyes of storefronts.

Age has a way of lining the safe of youth.

STILL ON MY LIPS

With each edition of *Leaves of Grass* till you died,

you practiced the art of censorship. First

self-published in 1855, your book, in disguise,

shouted the need for manly love and all that entailed.

Women were almost an afterthought. After 1860,

accusations of obscenity forced your right hand

to stop its unseemly shorthand of onanism.

You turned down the brass in "Song of Myself,"

castrating your tenor voice with your pen's scissors.

THE KISS OF WALT WHITMAN

Never mind the fact that men everywhere

wrote you letters of veiled want and worship.

One woman was even mistaken enough to move

from England to America in hopes of marriage!

Love in art became a compromising position,

caught with its pants down, mooning sweet ass.

Its bottom must submit to the top dollar,

straining in its ever-increasing impotency

to stay erect all the way to your deathbed.

STILL ON MY LIPS

Leaves of Grass had initially sprouted out of the mish-

mash of pithy lines scribbled in financial ledgers.

You'd cut and pasted clippings from here and there.

You didn't know what to do with them at first;

only when you returned from a trip to New Orleans,

where you met a man whose name is lost to all but you,

did you at last *see*: O passion! O sweet love! O America!

The wanton filth you self-published was a pink grenade

detonating in an atomic cloud straight from the future.

Although you claimed to love all people, all races,

the black community does not claim you as a hero.

You had once called freed blacks "baboons"

in one of your essays. No one saw you as a racist

back then; much like how Abraham Lincoln,

the Great Emancipator himself, had made

racist statements in his early political career.

Today no one would get away with these comments

uttered in public. Not everyone likes what you wrote.

STILL ON MY LIPS

You preferred language of the plainspoken.

Poetry had to be more accessible, more democratic.

You exulted in the exclamations of sex.

Yet you cloaked your unspeakable love in a language

that only others of your kind could translate.

They stole their way to your door, sometimes your bed.

You defended the right of young men to exercise

in public. Such perspiration provided inspiration

from the obscenities of your brain and groin.

THE KISS OF WALT WHITMAN

When someone confronted you with evidence

of you always loving young men intimately,

you claimed once to have sired five children.

Only five? You've fathered generations after generations!

So many look like you with a dozen mothers.

They've invented stories and legends about the father

they wish they'd known had you lived longer.

Your kisses have been quilted atop the DNA threads

of their hearts, so often bruised by love's needle.

STILL ON MY LIPS

The elderberry wine that passed between

you and Oscar Wilde is history,

a century absorbed in the bloodstream,

warming conversation in a long coat

gently slid off and left on the chair.

Two hours of words and nodding understanding.

Only you two know what you did.

Yet you left him enough of a kiss to brag.

Discretion, you would've warned. *Discretion!*

THE KISS OF WALT WHITMAN

When faced with a basketful of pictures

showing you evolving over the years, you said,

"I meet new Walt Whitmans every day."

You were something of an exhibitionist, weren't you,

relishing the importance of being photographed.

You knew that a single picture could accomplish more

far quickly than a single poem could.

The repetition of your eyes, beard, and face

has fossilized how we see you: an old man.

STILL ON MY LIPS

By the time your hair grayed at thirty,

you were already a Christ in training.

Then you exploded with orgasms of revelation.

In the prime of your forties, you stood tall,

fit as an ox and horny as a bull. You didn't trim

your locks. You knew you had to seem unkempt,

wild enough to inspire terror in the untamed.

You knew what lurked between their legs,

the untenable desire to master the body's scriptures.

THE KISS OF WALT WHITMAN

The original daguerrotype of you standing

with your hand on hip, gazing intently at us,

is lost. Samuel Hollyer created its lithographic

reproduction as the frontispiece image

for *Leaves of Grass*. It wasn't enough

to clothe beautiful obscenities with artful lines.

You had to have your phallic heft enlarged

for subsequent editions. You had to swagger

big as America, growing outward and upward.

Even Gavin Arthur, the author of *The Circle of Sex*,

detailed the time when your friend Edward Carpenter

demonstrated to him, complete with nuzzles and licks,

of how you and Eddy had sex, right down to your growls

emanating deep from the autumnal woods,

your spirit passing down to him, the next generation.

Moaning, Arthur thought: "Walt. Then him. Then me."

This has to be the rarest kind of oral history imaginable.

Shouldn't such secrets be kept sacred, off-limits?

THE KISS OF WALT WHITMAN

How much should we know of you, Walt?

We live in an age of gossip passing for news.

Boyd McDonald said, "People in show business are

in the business of showing themselves." Nude,

you posed in a Thomas Eakins photographic study

when you were in your sixties, profiling

fertile belly, burning bush, and dangling root.

No one knew it then, but you were already

America's first male celebrity centerfold.

STILL ON MY LIPS

Kindred comrades became more open in the 1970s,

ecstatic with discovery and affection

even in the flickering eight-millimeter blue films.

They smiled radiantly, dressed with warm caresses,

with arc lights heating the contours of bodies.

They were alive with the innocence of libido.

Being naked and hard on camera was still taboo.

Who knew that porn could be tender?

We weren't yet a nation of amateur centerfolds.

THE KISS OF WALT WHITMAN

What now, Walt, do you think of today's porn stars?

Their humongous cocks are perpetually stiff.

Never mind that most of us aren't well-hung.

Their sinewy bodies set new standards a few match.

Their chests, like their balls, are shaven.

They rarely smile at each other. No joy.

They're too busy grunting with ass in close-up.

Thanks to editing, they seem forever insatiable.

Sucking and fucking's just another factory job.

STILL ON MY LIPS

Nothing like Mr. Eakins's painting *The Swimming Hole*:

the suppleness of the six nude young men, golden

as the late afternoon sun discreetly caressing their asses,

their family jewels glittering in shadow of their pubes

as they stand and dive off a slag of bricked rocks,

a brown spaniel paddling toward one of the men

looking down in the mirror rippling his hidden face

as he reaches down into the waves if only to feel

the momentary thrill of cold on a fine summer day.

THE KISS OF WALT WHITMAN

At 330 Mickle Boulevard in Camden, New Jersey,

your house still stands, a tourist attraction.

I've never visited; always zipped through for New York.

Pictures online reveal the smallness of your daily life,

much like the cameos of men I've loved, frozen

in bas-relief. They are clothes impossible to rid of.

Alone in my bed I am unable to strip down to the boy

I used to be, then in awe of men in sweaty testosterone.

The bed you died in creaks a symphony of silence.

STILL ON MY LIPS

The old Camden County Jail once sat with square eyes

staring down with a red-brick muzzled jaw

right across the street from you. It's a ghost wiped clean.

Did you peer out your windows for inmates

freed that day in front of the prison's gates?

Empty lots near your house are littered with idle talk.

You dreamed of a city where men could love

and hold hands as intimates in the streets.

Isn't this what you'd always wanted, a crime-free love?

THE KISS OF WALT WHITMAN

O how you'd loved Harry Stoddard, 39 years

younger than you! Hank was your darling son,

exchanging rings with him and then hiding them.

You two posed for a picture, his ring showing.

But he was moody, jealous. You saw other young men.

Sometimes you demanded the return of his ring.

"I wish you would put the ring on my finger again."

You wanted it all—domestic love and sexual bliss

with all who'd lusted for a daddy in their fantasies.

STILL ON MY LIPS

How far away from the prying eyes of his family

did you two have to go on his father's farm to kiss,

embrace, and sigh into each other's eyes?

You sunbathed in the nude with him on Timber Creek.

Today the Internet lists locations of nudist beaches,

showing snapshots of men and women wrapping arms

around each other without the slightest shyness.

Isn't that what you'd envisioned of the future?

America's changed a lot since you left.

III.

His beautiful body is borne
    in the circling eddies,
it is continually bruised on rocks,
Swiftly and out of sight is borne
    the brave corpse.

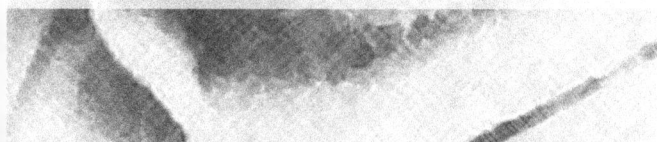

THE KISS OF WALT WHITMAN

Enemy rain machine-gunned the windows.

My front line of soldier-plants survived.

The battlefield below dripped green with blood.

The gray skies hung heavy with loss.

Flags were not lowered to half-mast.

No one delivered eulogies for the severed leaves,

littering cemetery plots along the sidewalk.

A procession of white crosses did not march.

Each barren tree stretched its arms up to God.

STILL ON MY LIPS

You interviewed one soldier after another

on the horrors of the War against Slavery,

a gut-wrenching squabble over color.

You saw their gaping amputations,

the blood-shot madness in their eyes.

You heard their babble of whiskey and pain.

You smelled their chloroform of defeat.

You held their hands and made promises.

You loved them all. The Potomac flowed blood.

THE KISS OF WALT WHITMAN

No one writes about the dead anymore.

The fear of infection and loss isn't so dramatic now.

Pills are today's answer to everything.

Each month brings us new findings,

often conflicting with each other. No matter.

Progress, progress is being steadily made!

My last friend who died of AIDS went ten years ago.

Nowadays men advertise condom-free encounters.

Death's now a punch line to a joke that no one gets.

STILL ON MY LIPS

Things were simpler for men like us in your time.

Either you married and had sex on the side,

or you lived alone as a bachelor at a boardinghouse.

"The right woman" was always a hookah dream.

Information about your kind was suspect.

It was always about the eyes mirroring desire.

Sometimes love of the rough kind grew,

but there wasn't a recognized word for it.

Love was the far more obscene word.

THE KISS OF WALT WHITMAN

In my time love provided all my oxygen.

I breathed the capillaries of my first love,

coupling endlessly and spooning afterwards.

My lungs were robust like Vikings at sea.

I could spray shooting stars late at night!

We leaped about the waves at Rehoboth Beach

in the graying July sun. Pitch-perfect.

I told everyone that I was a comrade of men.

But when my first love left me, I needed an iron lung.

STILL ON MY LIPS

Alone in the asylum I stared, trying not to vomit

when far too many patients lined up,

the purple splotches tattooing their stick arms

reaching out for God, Allah, Zeus—anyone!

Their craggy faces cried surrender

to the rivulets of toxins slithering like snakes

inside their skins, swelling pus by the hour.

But I was no Florence Nightingale.

I was too scared of quarantine with *them*.

THE KISS OF WALT WHITMAN

In those days, no one could figure out anything.
These dying men became a circus of experiments,
one toxic drug trial after another. Nurses wouldn't
enter their rooms with their trays of food. I saw
friends wither away like bitter rosebushes in winter.
I fought nights not to masturbate. What if I'd sown
within me the seeds of my own mortality?
Mornings I found my body outlined in sweaty salts
on my black futon sheets, the scene of a crime.

Should I go, Walt, before I'm ready to depart,

one look I but gave, which your dear eyes return'd,

please cradle me as you would another soldier,

one touch of your hand to mine, O boy, reach'd up

so I could look up into your eyes tender,

on the earth partially reclining, sat by your side.

For if die alone I must, there must be someone

in the night reliev'd, to the place at last,

where men sing eulogies of heaven-sent orgasm.

Instead I found you asleep on your side,

against the forgiving moss spreading

under the sycamores on the Capitol grounds.

You were exhausted from these interviews

injecting morphine of nightmares into your brain.

You were addicted to loving them, their final hour.

I looked up and saw men limping, making-do

with handmade crutches, their leg stumps

a reminder of the miles they'd marched.

STILL ON MY LIPS

Heads bowed, they gathered around you.

I kept searching their faces, wondering

if they too had clandestine sex with you.

One of them gave me an angry stare. *What?*

"He's dead now." You were a statue of peace.

No one cried. They had no tears left.

I lay down next to you, stroking your face.

You'd been paralyzed dead for over a century.

Your beard in my hands crumbled into ivy vines.

THE KISS OF WALT WHITMAN

Its dusty feet took root. The fray of your beard

spread like a virus unstoppable on its quest,

meshing deep into the ground.

The men gasped decades-pent cries of orgasm

as they collapsed into the humping ground.

Your body was soon knotted in hairy vines

until you were one with the grass fingers cornholing

for more. I was levitated in a bed of aura.

The air hung with incandescent sperm.

STILL ON MY LIPS

Inhaling deeply the musk of bodies arising

from the earth, I licked the air for more sweat.

Their translucent spirits floated around me.

I reached out to touch them but I felt the absence

of warmth pulsating in their veins. I tasted ice

chips melting on my tongue. They felt like tears

bleeding, slithering into the darkest crevices

of my body. Gazing into their eyes I saw a river

with no ties to the ocean, no relief in sight.

THE KISS OF WALT WHITMAN

Your face mushroomed out of the clouds,

killing me with the kindness in your eyes.

You blew a gust of wind, flinging me far

above the trees into the Potomac River

sluggish with the buzz of mosquitoes

the color of crimson. Was it safe to swim?

I'd been afraid of the one fatal kiss,

infections swimming upstream like salmon

in my blood. No matter. I was drowning.

STILL ON MY LIPS

Helpless, I gulped the Potomac's blood and semen,

death and life in the same breath. A wisp

out of control, I spun with vultures circling,

following my feverishness to the river's mouth

vomiting sewage into the great Atlantic Ocean.

I clawed at the salty waves until a huge one slapped me

north to the shore where the Pilgrims once stood.

I rolled over in a foam of seaweed and discarded tins.

I wept. So you didn't want this driftwood either!

THE KISS OF WALT WHITMAN

These Pilgrims had wanted you burnt at the stake

long before you were born. No one should sex!

Wearing a splash of color was akin to carnal knowledge.

No one else wanted their stern ideas of the universe

so they had to find a land where there was no one

with besotted ideas of what a proper religion should be.

Their bones brittled resolve for God's sake.

Laughter and lust would be carefully rationed.

The only wood left burning was made of accusations.

STILL ON MY LIPS

You were the first radical faerie, a pagan

whose chants committed the joyful sin of blasphemy.

You never sided with any religion. All were equal.

You posed in a slovenly suit from time to time.

You let your hair grow out scraggly.

Sometimes you left the top of your shirt open.

Such witchcraft of comradeship beat in your chest,

ravens fluttering to the stars and shaking loose twigs

into a pyre. I offer you the match. Strike me.

IV.

Whatever goes to the tilth of me
it shall be you,
You my rich blood, your milky stream
pale strippings of my life.

THE KISS OF WALT WHITMAN

There's no genteel bohemia left in Mannahatta.

Your specimen days of comradeship are gone;

the sweet understanding of us against them

is not enough to adhere us together as one.

Nothing like Pfaff's, that bar on Bleecker and Broadway,

where you met all sorts of characters and writers.

People in the know knew it as a semi-gay bar.

How sweet it must've been to find each other,

the fruit of loins ripened for the picking!

STILL ON MY LIPS

You attracted one young man after another.

They must've seemed plentiful like weeds,

awkward and clumsy with inchoate desire.

You plucked them clean, sowing them into flowers

in full bloom, their memories of you an eternal spring

by the time the nectar of love dried up.

You bounced from one to another like a bee,

gathering up honey for the world to share.

My hands offer only rotting exoskeletons.

THE KISS OF WALT WHITMAN

He and I talk less and less on the phone.

It's no longer spring when possibilities wafted,

when a pillow next to me was him in my arms.

The windows toss winds among my houseplants,

taller and stronger than when I bought them

with him at the garden store a few months before.

Each morning I'd tended them with water,

the essential liquid of my heart still hoping.

I catch the fragrance of winter ready to break.

STILL ON MY LIPS

My remaining courage is that of a seed

gutted deep in the parched skin of Death Valley.

The pendulum of sun gives the same answer.

The question of water is nonsense.

Not even a cloud is willing to let its faucet drip.

Underground, vermin sniff my loneliness

and scurry away. I'm not even tasty.

The dust of decay mothballs my outer shell.

I'm a skeleton in search of a heart. Water me.

THE KISS OF WALT WHITMAN

I'm so tired of all this crap, Walt. Hum me a lullaby.

Allow me to sleep beside you, your sure hand

stroking my back gently as a summer breeze,

kisses tender as bees inspecting for nectar,

beard flowing cascades of forget-me-nots,

belly rafting up and down like an ocean,

eyelids a tree shade of dreams best untold,

heart beating to the orchestra of crickets

tuning up for the great symphony of summer.

STILL ON MY LIPS

Young men were idealized in your time.

You hung photographs of them cavorting

in an anonymous pond somewhere in Vermont.

Odd that no one thought men of a certain age sexy,

grays and whites creeping the vestigial wrinkles of youth,

if not more than these lithe twinks, a dime a dozen

in peep booth videos. Sex has lost its mysticism,

its wanton mysteries exposed like a magician's secrets.

How the hell can I compete with the body I have?

THE KISS OF WALT WHITMAN

My body naked full of landmines is this:

explosions of tiny freckles underneath my face,

no trace of a flesh-colored mole shaved off my nose,

a cleft in chin hidden in the tangle of beard,

a tiny toad wart on my right index finger,

a trio of gallbladder removal scars under ribcage,

a shiny knee patch from a scooter accident,

my back covered with the poison ivy of fur.

Who'd want to sleep with this scarred creature?

STILL ON MY LIPS

In the dark, I dream of singing like Marietta Alboni,

an opera singer you worshiped. Her voice was velvet,

encasing the finger-veins of your heart like gloves,

No recording of her voice exists, but yours does,

allegedly. You spoke the first four lines of "America"

for Thomas Edison. No one can confirm

if it's indeed *you* speaking. My memories

spiral over and over again on wax cylinders.

But each piece of music can last only so long.

THE KISS OF WALT WHITMAN

These here are undeveloped rolls of memory:

an inconsequential note written in his hand,

a frayed flannel shirt in spring pastels,

a precious email printout, a home video saved to disc,

a discontinued IKEA bedside lamp shade,

a newspaper clipping with a phrase highlighted in ink,

the first movie we saw together in the theater,

a receipt from the restaurant where we first met.

Sentimentality's a garage sale. No one's buying.

STILL ON MY LIPS

Please talk to him, Walt. My muse's been an asshole.

He won't put out ideas for me. I'm a has-been.

He's a starfucker, an opportunist. I've been had

with his promises of deeper knowledge,

a greater command of the universe.

I'm left with stale peanuts. My muse knows

how badly I need inspiration, the ultimate fuck.

He says I got bad breath. This relationship's over.

All I've got left are promises that nobody wants.

THE KISS OF WALT WHITMAN

If only I could rescue you from your family crypt

and blow a magic kiss there into your dormant lungs:

awakening, you'd look bewildered up into my eyes,

dark as elderberries and the oceans yet to be,

and find your creaky body rolling back to the age of 36,

once a frustrated newspaper editor now filled with vigor

when you typeset some of the twelve poems, not yet

titled, for *Leaves of Grass*, a tiny handbook showing

how to celebrate America through your body.

STILL ON MY LIPS

I'd take you in hand and bring you to my quiet laptop,

scrolling down its plethora of fonts—no longer limited

by the metal types available on hand—and easily

laying out text, deleting, pasting, tweaking margins.

You'd grip my shoulder, exclaiming the gee-whizzery

at lines matter-of-factly depicting men having sex.

No bloody ink stains on my hands. My keyboard is clean.

You'd fall down to your knees, blubbering of miracles.

Get up, Walt. We comrades still have a far way to go.

THE KISS OF WALT WHITMAN

The Internet is the bathhouse of the 21st century.

There's no romance left in efficient texting.

We're sometimes afraid to show our imperfect faces,

so we red-flag our erections, the only bragging right

that counts. Everything gets stated upfront.

The one-night stand is a *pre*-prenuptial agreement.

We've reduced ourselves to pixels and numbers,

touching cock but never another human being.

We're just dust, ghosts flickering on the screen.

STILL ON MY LIPS

Days of sitting still for a photograph have evaporated

into your hand, into a tiny gizmo unimagined

in the science fictions of Jules Verne, a handful

of saucer-eyed colors and bouncing images.

You master quickly the science of tapping that button,

disbelieving its lack of photographic plates,

the absence of bulky lenses and tripods and cloths

cloaking the bulk of photographer barking, *Stay still!*

You are stunned by your face in color on the screen.

THE KISS OF WALT WHITMAN

Color? More than a century ago you dreamed of fame

in grayscale replicated across dots of newsprint;

you were a reporter cursed with a poet's heart.

You posed for pictures as often as possible: 128 of them

survive. Only Lincoln had two more pictures than you!

You wanted everyone to memorize the contours

of your face, your eyes piercing through the glass.

You loved autographing pictures of yourself.

It meant you existed! Their avowals were poetry.

STILL ON MY LIPS

A clatter and clang from all directions lands you

back on lower Broadway, where you used to cruise

men fresh off the docks, streetcars, horses.

Mannahatta smells strangely clean: no horseshit,

no brace of sea salt-peppered winds off the docks,

no nose-itches from people who'd bathed only weekly.

The hum of factories and the pump of coal smoke are

no more. Cars, taxis, and buses brake, groan, honk.

Cobblestones are paved in black; sidewalks, concrete.

THE KISS OF WALT WHITMAN

The new buildings are not timid and dull-colored.

Its walls sheen with pristine glass, mirroring the skies

and skyscrapers taller than the Tower of Babel.

You spot a huge metal log with knife-wings spread out

coasting among the clouds. What the jig is *that*?

Why isn't anyone watching *that*—a huge bird!—flying?

Why isn't anyone shouting newspaper headlines?

People aim their little screens at the Brooklyn Bridge.

No one seems amazed by the things they photograph.

STILL ON MY LIPS

Young muscular men in tank tops brandish tattoos.
Coiffed women in halter tops, shorts, and neon shoes
groove to tiny white bits of music inside their ears.
Whatever happened to long dresses? Coats? Hats?
So much naked skin—*in public?*—is jawdropping.
If they looked up from their palm-screens, they'd spot
the wide-eyed wonder and goofy grin on your face
at this mind-blowing spectacle passing right on by.
You take another selfie. You're still *so* American.

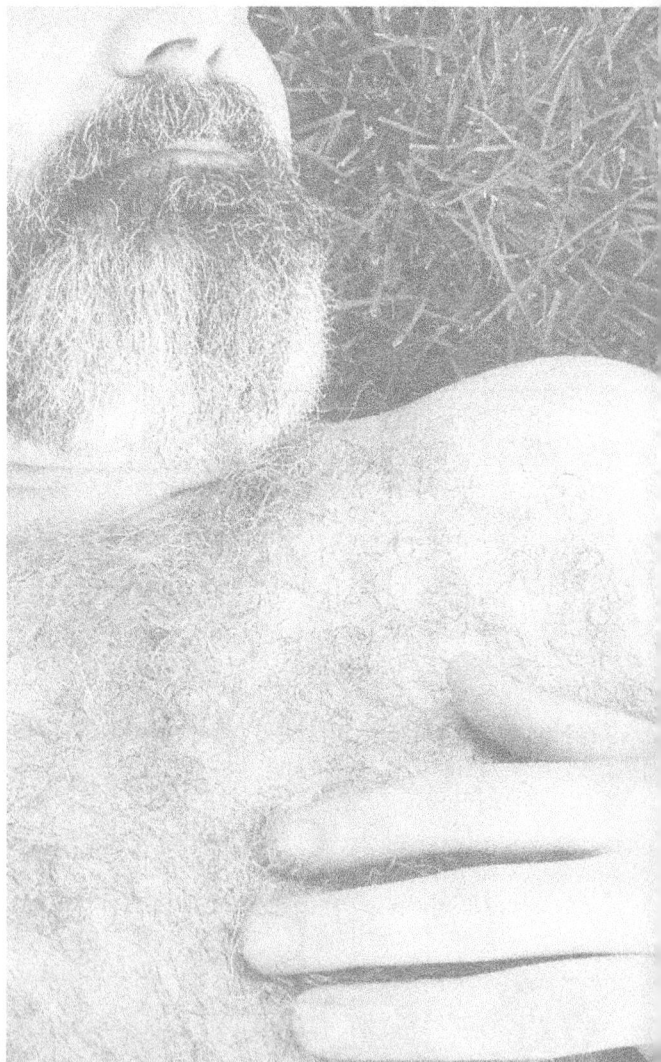

V.

I saw in Louisiana a live-oak growing,
All alone stood it, and the moss hung down
from the branches,
Without any companion it grew there...

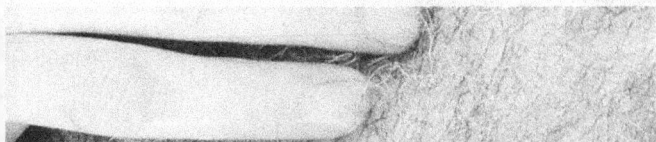

THE KISS OF WALT WHITMAN

I dream of catching you, Walt, on the smoking patio

behind the Minneapolis Eagle. You'd wear a t-shirt,

jeans and sandals; hold up a pint of lager in your hand.

Kiss me in front of everyone. How could I resist

the you, that sexy doe-eyed man, your hand to chin,

who Mathew Brady had photographed a few times?

My desire breaks out in beads of sweat. I must leave.

The sound of your phone vibrating startles you.

It's me texting you: *Can you stay with me tonight?*

STILL ON MY LIPS

Gone! the milkweed, songs of monarch butterflies.

Gone! the fingers of grasses harping on the wind.

Gone! the rumble of ants strip-mining the earth.

Gone! the scatter of raccoons toppling garbage cans.

Gone! the summer days of symphony and silence.

My voice! a broken Stradivarius. I've lost its bow.

It's winter. My heart is a frozen tundra. It's all gone.

The long dark months can only shroud my ache.

A daily hour of sun will be enough for me to pretend.

THE KISS OF WALT WHITMAN

Walt, you walked among men and women,

inhaling all their unfettered breaths.

You performed mouth-to-mouth resuscitation,

daring them to feel your tongue swirling

more passion, shuddering there on the loam,

a bed filled with earthworms and ants and rot.

Rain drops of sweat fell from their bodies,

watering so much that they too drowned.

They were mere houseplants. You were a Sequoia!

STILL ON MY LIPS

With long hair and flowing beard, you waded like Moses

in a sea of these soldiers, some dismembered,

amidst the infirmary abuzz with flies and cries.

Everywhere the burning bushes whispered morphine.

Your eyes spoke commandments of tenderness,

aching to make love to these mortal gods,

but instead you took dictation on your tablets,

your pen dipped in blood from their inkwells.

Each day when you left, the Red Sea parted before you.

THE KISS OF WALT WHITMAN

Please rescue me from the sterility of America.

Everything's been shrink-wrapped and digitized.

I can't touch or feel anything real. Damn*piss*shit*fuck*.

It's all up here, not down here or there.

It's all commercials and franchises.

Even death has its own antiseptic soap dispenser.

Advertisers use sex as their biological weapon.

Demographics are a communal sport of saturation.

Christ! Just scrape the ISBN bar code off my DNA.

STILL ON MY LIPS

In loam rich to home which all must return,

I lay myself down to slumber eternal.

The white drone of television lurks behind me,

marking each Nielsen hour of canned laughter

a tragedy best unheard in the cemetery.

I rest on my side, fidgeting on an unmade bed,

wondering elegies for each kiss unfulfilled.

I'm a sleepwalker bumping into dreams,

him already lost in the land of the undead.

THE KISS OF WALT WHITMAN

Long after I've caught him, the ghost of my affections,

trapping him into the crypt of what'll never happen,

I will cease visiting his memory in the graveyard.

I will leave behind insipid vases of fake flowers,

forgetting that gravediggers will clear them away

before winter. Each visit with him undead

will be a séance of conjuring up what we first saw

in each other the first time we rose out of earth,

avoiding the Ouija board of questions never answered.

STILL ON MY LIPS

One night a dream handsome and lonesome will slip

beside me underneath the shivery sheets,

stitch his arms around me as you have,

kite the key of kisses at the lightning of bygones,

thundering me past what you've taught me,

a mere apprentice in your unorthodox ways.

That beautiful shadow will announce himself,

a scientist in the spirituality of our bodies electric.

I lie on the slab, awaiting his jolt of volt——

THE KISS OF WALT WHITMAN

No, no, no! Throttle this corpse of me alive:

Let the rags of hypocrisy fall away:

Map me naked your atlas of desire:

Sow this soil over with kisses:

Let the sun of your eyes warm my leafy thighs:

Sprinkle me with the dew of your tongue:

Inhale me!

No sweeter embrace than yours:

I'm forever awash in your . . .

STILL ON MY LIPS

O pulse of my life!

O drops of me!

Earth! My likeness!

O blossoms of my blood!

O the magnet!

O burning and throbbing—

The scent of these arm-pits is aroma finer than prayer.

Loveflesh swelling and deliciously aching whiteblood.

limitless jets of love, hot and enormous . . .

THE KISS OF WALT WHITMAN

With your kiss lingering on my lips, I will sample

here and there in the dark and the daylight

the mouths and bodies and hearts of men

who, too, are looking for that gossamer thread

woven stronger than sweat and sperm.

They are looking for their own Walt Whitmans.

Out there is a new wilderness of bramble.

Hope and courage will power my chainsaw.

As I wend my way, patience must stay precious as water.

STILL ON MY LIPS

On the brightest of mornings, he will pluck weeds

from my heart, long composted and unrecognizable.

With his eyes locked upon my purpled tulip,

its glistening stamen awaiting the flurry of bees,

he will wonder whose nectar is left on my tongue.

I will shock him with my voiceless hands signing arias,

its seed-milk budding from the kisses of a new man.

O veiny stem! O sweet dew! O what magnificence!

Water borne of love is the sweetest blood of the earth.

Acknowledgments

Excerpts from this book have been previously published under these titles:

Art & Understanding: "Two Decades and Then Some."

Assaracus: A Journal of Gay Poetry: "Bound at the Stake."

Between: New Gay Poetry (Jameson Currier, ed.; Chelsea Station Editions): "The Dinner Guest."

Chautauqua Literary Review: "Recital."

RFD Magazine: "Bodies Cavorting," "Centerfolds," and "The Other Moses."

PHOTOGRAPH: M. NICOLAS SILVA

About the Author

Raymond Luczak is the author and editor of 18 books. Titles include *How to Kill Poetry*, *Mute*, and *This Way to the Acorns*. His Deaf gay novel *Men with Their Hands* won first place in the Project: QueerLit Contest 2006. His work has been nominated three times for the Pushcart Prize. He lives in Minneapolis, Minnesota. [raymondluczak.com]

"I meet new Walt Whitmans every day."

www.ingramcontent.com/pod-product-compliance
Lightning Source LLC
Chambersburg PA
CBHW021624270326
41931CB00008B/858